Jack
and the Beanstalk

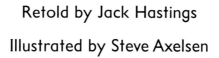

Retold by Jack Hastings

Illustrated by Steve Axelsen

alphakids

Once upon a time there was a boy called Jack.

He lived with his mother in a little house.
They were very poor and hungry.
All they had was a cow.

'We'll have to sell the cow so we can buy some
food,' said Jack's mother. 'Take her to market
and make sure you get a good price.'

Jack was walking to the market when a man passed by.

'What a lovely cow,' he said to Jack.

'I'm going to the market to sell her,' said Jack.

'I will swap these magic beans for your cow,' said the man.

'Magic beans?' thought Jack. 'What could be a better price for our cow? My mother will be so pleased with me!'

But when he got home and showed his mother the beans, she was furious. 'You silly boy!' she cried. 'You sold our only cow for a handful of useless beans. What are we going to do now?'

And she threw the beans out of the window.

Jack went to bed hungry and sad.

When he woke up in the morning, there was an enormous beanstalk outside his window.
It was so tall that Jack could not see the top.

Jack climbed out his window and up the beanstalk. He climbed up and up and up.

When he got to the top of the beanstalk, Jack was high above the clouds. In front of him was a huge house.

Jack crept inside the house. He followed the smell of food and soon found himself in the kitchen. The tallest woman he had ever seen was busy roasting chickens and stirring large pots of lamb stew. Jack hid behind an enormous saucepan.

All of a sudden the ground started to shake.
Jack trembled in his hiding place.

A giant appeared in the doorway. He sniffed
the air and roared, 'Fee! Fi! Fo! Fum! I can smell
a little one!'

'Don't be silly,' said the woman to the giant.
'There aren't any children here. Sit down and
eat your lunch.'

The giant ate four chickens and two pots of lamb stew for lunch.

Then the giant picked up a little harp.

'Play!' said the giant to the harp.
The harp played a tune.
Jack was amazed that the harp could play by itself.

Then the woman brought in a white goose.

'Lay!' said the giant to the goose.
The goose laid a golden egg.
Jack was amazed that eggs could be made of gold.

Soon the giant fell asleep.

Jack ran out of the house and climbed down the beanstalk as fast as he could.

Jack's mother was waiting for him at the bottom, looking cross.

She didn't believe a word he said about magic harps that played on their own or geese that laid golden eggs.

'Useless old beans and a useless beanstalk,' was all she said.

The next day Jack climbed back up the beanstalk and hid in the giant's kitchen.

The ground started to shake and the giant appeared in the doorway. He sniffed the air.

'Fee! Fi! Fo! Fum! I can smell a little one!' he roared.

Jack trembled at the giant's words.

'I think you must have a cold,' said the woman. 'There aren't any children here. Sit down and eat your dinner.'

The giant ate an enormous dinner.

Jack waited until the giant fell asleep.

When the air started to rumble with giant snores, Jack picked up the goose and the harp and ran out of the house as fast as his legs would carry him.

'Master, master!' the harp cried out to the sleeping giant.

The giant woke up and chased after Jack.

Jack climbed down the beanstalk as quickly as he could. When he got to the bottom he chopped down the beanstalk and ran inside to find his mother.

Jack took the golden eggs to the market
and sold them for lots of money.

Now Jack and his mother never go to bed hungry.

The harp plays its beautiful tunes for them
every night. And Jack's mother has not said
another word about useless old beans.